CW01064631

GOD'S GRACE KEPT ME

Lessons on How Staying Close to God
Can Help You Achieve Your Dreams,
Discover Your Greatness, and Lead You
Toward Your Destiny

JENNIFER DIXON

WESTBOW
PRESS®
A DIVISION OF THOMAS NELSON
& ZONDERVAN

WestBow Press books may be ordered through booksellers or by contacting:

WestBow Press
A Division of Thomas Nelson & Zondervan
1663 Liberty Drive
Bloomington, IN 47403
www.westbowpress.com
844-714-3454

Scripture quotations marked ESV taken from The Holy Bible, English Standard Version® (ESV®), Copyright © 2001 by Crossway, a publishing ministry of Good News Publishers. All rights reserved.

Scripture quotations marked KJV are taken from the King James Version.

ISBN: 979-8-3850-1318-0 (sc)
ISBN: 979-8-3850-1319-7 (hc)
ISBN: 979-8-3850-1317-3 (e)

Library of Congress Control Number: 2023922485

Print information available on the last page.

WestBow Press rev. date: 07/25/2024

"For by grace you have been saved through faith. And this is not your own doing; it is the gift of God" (Ephesians 2:8 ESV).

Dear God,

I thank you for your grace. I don't know where I'd be if you weren't in my life. You have kept me through it all, even when I wasn't sure of what to do or how I was going to make it through. You picked me up, held my hand, gave me unconditional love, encouraged my heart, stayed by my side, and guided me toward my purpose. And for that, I am grateful. I love you so much. You are mine. I am yours. Forever and ever.

—Jennifer

Dedication

To the person who has ever felt like you did not have a purpose, God is always shining His light on you.

Contents

Preface

This is it. It is the moment I have been waiting for. I can feel myself getting more and more anxious and then … the music begins. As I entered the auditorium, I was excited because in just a few hours, I'd be receiving my master's degree in English. After listening to powerful commencement speeches, it was finally time to distribute the diplomas. I am so nervous, and my heart is beating extremely fast. There's a big crowd. What if I drop my diploma? What if they start to laugh? I looked to my left and saw my sister, holding both her and my mom's phones, trying to take a quick photo. A few graduates were standing in front of me. While waiting to hear my name, I remember thinking, *Here we go, Jennifer. There's no turning back now.*

I inched a bit closer to the stage with my wheelchair and stopped on the black "x" on the floor. Moments later, I drove up the ramp and gave my name card to the faculty member who was announcing the "master of arts" students. When she announced my name into the microphone, the entire auditorium started screaming, cheering, and clapping for me. While on stage, I looked out into the crowd. I couldn't believe the response. All these people were cheering for me, and I just took a minute to allow it to sink in. Then, the university president handed me my diploma, the photographer took our photo, and I left the stage. So many people were smiling and congratulating me as I went back to my seat. I sat there in awe because I actually did it. Every all-nighter, every paper, every discussion, every presentation, every assignment was worth celebrating. I loved sharing my success with family, friends, and those who have motivated and helped me get to where I am today.

Once the ceremony was over, I waited in the auditorium to see my family (my mom, dad, sister, and grandma) and take photos with them. Suddenly, a sweet gentleman walked up to me with the biggest smile on his face. He was wearing a gray and black plaid buttoned-up shirt with light gray suit pants and black shoes. He hugged me tight and gave me a peck on the cheek. I didn't know him, but I thought it was a kind gesture. Then he said, "I just wanted to say that you have inspired me so much today. I'm even considering going back to school. I'm so proud of you." I replied, "Thank you," and we smiled at each other.

Smiling has always been a natural form of communication for me. I often receive a lot of compliments on my smile, and it's usually the first thing that people notice. There have been countless times when I was approached by random individuals or family members who say, "You have the prettiest smile," "You are always smiling," or "Never stop flashing that beautiful smile." My bus attendant in first grade even gave me the nickname "smiley" and greeted me with such happiness every morning. His name was John. He was an older man, probably in his late fifties, early sixties, with white hair. He was sweet to everyone, especially me. He never called me Jennifer, and it irked me a bit, like why was he so cheery when I got on the bus? Then I asked my mom what she thought. She said, "You make him happy, Jenny." Being a kid, I didn't understand how much of an influence I had on John. It never crossed my mind that he could have been going through a tumultuous situation, and my smile made him forget about all his worries, and maybe my presence brightened his day. The next day, I remembered what my mom told me. As soon as John saw me, his face beamed with joy, and that is when I realized she was right! I did make John happy, and it felt wonderful to know that I could embolden his heart. I believe it's the reason I still smile now—to be a ray of light, spread positivity, and let others know that we can't control every circumstance, but we can choose how to handle the situation. We can either feel sorry for ourselves, or we can keep pushing and smile until something amazing happens. I'm choosing happiness. Which one are you going to pick?! Like John, I had a profound effect on the gentleman at my graduation as well, and I'm so grateful for that moment. His comments meant the world to me because not only did I inspire him, but he reminded me of just how far I've come.

Let's take a little trip down memory lane with some photos.

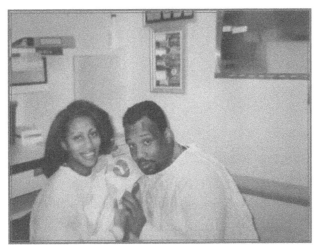

Happy birthday, Jennifer! Here's a picture of my parents holding me for the first time at the hospital. God's Grace is in full effect.

*Here's a close-up picture of my dad and me.
Didn't I look like a sweet baby doll?*

This is a picture of me and my family when I was little. My parents with their three beautiful girls— you'll get to know more about them in a bit.

I love this photo! I feel like it captures the essence of who I am—someone who is always smiling, laughing, and finding the joy in everything. If I could give any advice to this little girl, I'd say "Keep shining, Jennifer! You are going to bless and inspire so many throughout your journey."

This is a photo of me standing in my walker. Go, Jenny, go!

This was picture day, maybe third or fourth grade.
Awww. See, I told you smiling just comes naturally.

*This is a photo of me when I graduated with
my associate's degree in English!*

This is a photo of my baby and me. She will always be one of the greatest gifts God ever gave to me. My sweet girl.

This is a photo of me when I graduated with my bachelor's degree in English with a minor in communication! Check out my Honor Society cords.

Here I am competing for the title of Ms. Wheelchair Illinois 2018, where I was the runner-up! This was my first pageant, and I was so proud of myself for taking that leap of faith and using my voice to share my story.

This photo was taken on the day I received my
master's degree in English. It is and will always
be one of the happiest moments of my life.

I was born with cerebral palsy (twenty-eight weeks premature).
I weighed two pounds five and a half ounces. I was so small
that I could fit into the palms of my dad's hands. My mom
always emphasized how little I was when looking through my
baby photos. She would say, "Look how little you were, Jenny."
Doctors told my parents that I would not be able to achieve many
things such as talking, walking, feeding myself, etc. Although my
parents were devastated by the diagnosis, they believed that God
could turn any situation around. After being in the hospital for
about four months, God answered their prayers, and my parents
were able to bring me home.

Growing up in a Christian household and living with a
disability, I was always determined. I worked hard at every task

presented before me such as feeding myself, brushing my teeth, learning how to write and spell my name, and getting excellent grades in school. The road to achieving my goals wasn't an easy one. I experienced a lot of ups and downs. I cried. I even felt like giving up many times, but the one thing that kept me going was my love for music. For the longest time, music has always been an enormous part of my journey. It was in my household daily. I have my dad to thank for that. He introduced me to gospel groups such as the Mighty Clouds of Joy, the Canton Spirituals, the Hawkins Family, and more. My dad also loved singing, which he inherited from his father. They even sang together in my granddad's group called the Original Redeemers when I was about ten years old. My dad taught me everything he knew about singing, from holding a single note to breathing from my diaphragm, harmonizing, and the importance of rehearsing. I learned so much about music from him, which is why it is such an essential part of who I am.

Music has uplifted and empowered me through some of the greatest and most difficult times in my life and taught me valuable lessons along the way. Music gave me reassurance that I could accomplish my dreams, and I wanted to share my passion with others. So, I created JMotivates (Jennifer Motivates) on Instagram. With my platform, I can connect and encourage not just my favorite artists but other creatives striving to make their dreams a reality. I've also been blessed to meet some of those artists whom I've admired for years such as Syleena Johnson, Lalah Hathaway, MAJOR., and Mary Mary. Above all, I intend on using my love for music and writing to motivate and help others recognize their full potential.

Here's a picture of Mary Mary and I backstage at their concert in 2013. I'll never forget that day. These women forever changed my life, and I'll share how a little later.

All these memories started coming back when the gentleman spoke to me after my graduation. He made me realize that I am impacting so many people with my life, and that is what matters most. I often say that if I can motivate or inspire at least one person, then I have done my job. He also reminded me that my disability does not define me. I can achieve amazing things if I trust God and believe in myself. Today, I want you to know that whether you have a disability or have experienced many hardships in your life, you have the power to achieve your dreams, too. Why? It is because you are strong and smart. You also never know who will be uplifted or impacted by your story. So, it is always important to keep God first, stay positive, work hard, and make a difference.

This book begins with one of my greatest accomplishments, chronicling my journey of how I conquered many challenges to reach an abundance of success. I am going to be very authentic when re-counting my life experiences with you. I want you to understand the depths of my heart and the extent of my struggles. I desire to show you how I turned every test into triumph and lead you toward your victory.

My purpose is to not only encourage those who have disabilities or are wheelchair users, but each one of you reading these words right now. Have you ever faced a challenge? Did you have moments where you felt like giving up but kept going? Are you currently feeling alone and don't know what direction to take? If you answered yes to any of these questions, then this book is for you. A lot of times when we are on our various journeys, we just need a little encouragement to help us along the way.

That is why I'm so excited to share important lessons from my life as well as songs that I listen to on my personal playlist. Each of the core messages that I've learned or sang along to inspired me to persevere, go outside of my comfort zone, and build a stronger relationship with God. I am just speaking my truth. I only want to give you what God has given me. I don't have all the answers, but what I do know from my own experiences and those around me is that God can perform miracles. I am one of them. Once you apply what I've provided, you will begin to see God work in your life too. I hope that as you read each story, you begin to realize that there are no limits when it comes to achieving your goals and that your dreams matter. You are unstoppable.

Now, it is important that before we start navigating through this journey together, I tell you what you can expect. I've compiled my thoughts into three simple components. First, this book is designed to help you remain optimistic when facing adversities. Even when life doesn't go as planned, you can still see the light at the end of the tunnel. Second, I know I wouldn't have gotten this far without God, and this book displays how utilizing your faith can strengthen you and give you a boost to keep moving forward. Finally, get ready to be motivated. This book will lift your spirits and have you feeling like you can conquer anything life throws at you.

As you delve into each chapter, I ask that you examine them thoroughly because I don't want you to miss out on the blessings that God has for you. You don't have to read the book all in one sitting, but I do encourage you to reflect on the words that are on each page, be willing to listen to what God has to say, and start preparing yourself for what's to come. God is about to change your life!

If you find yourself still needing more encouragement after our journey is finished, don't worry. I've got a special treat for you. At the end of each chapter, be sure to check out the God's Grace Kept Me Playlist. These are songs that I believe will keep you motivated as you go about your daily life. It is currently available on <u>YouTube</u>, <u>Amazon Music</u>, <u>Spotify</u>, and <u>Apple Music</u> so you can access and listen to the songs at your own convenience. Every song mentioned in this book has played a pivotal role in my life and touched my heart. I pray the same happens for you. I still go back to listen to them when I need to be uplifted.

I've got a feeling that this is going to be a life-changing experience! Are you prepared to take the next step closer toward your destiny? If you're reading this, you have passed your first test. See, I knew you could do it. Now, buckle your seatbelts, and let's make this an adventure you'll never forget.

Love, Appreciation, and Gratitude

When I am blessed with the opportunity to meet or be surrounded by people who have had an enormous impact on my life, I feel that it is always important to thank them for their support. I would like to take a minute to express my heartfelt gratitude right now.

To my mom, thank you for always believing in me and being there. You are the greatest mom any girl could ask for, dream of, and want in her life. I love you so much, and I only hope to be as wonderful and amazing as you one day. As for my dad, thank you for instilling in me my love for music.

To my Gram, thank you for all the laughs and love. You are the best, and I thank God for you. To my Grandma Rosie, you have continued to cover me with your love and prayers. I am so thankful; I love you. To my Granddad Frank, there is never a dull moment when you are in the room—from watching you passionately slam your cards down on the table when you play, to singing one of your favorite quartet songs, or your random outbursts. I can always count on you to make me laugh. Thank you. I love you. And to my Granddad Tommie Williams, I miss you so much, but I know you would be so proud of the woman I have become.

To my sister Jan, you are always willing to help me with whatever I need, whether it is carrying me over your shoulder when we go places, ordering our signature food—pizza—or just coming to chill. Thank you so much. I love you. And to my sister Jess, thank you for making me an auntie and blessing me with my amazing niece and nephew, Elise (Titi) and Erick (Bud). They have brought so much joy to my heart, and I love them so much.

To the many friends who have uplifted, encouraged, and empowered me throughout my journey, I appreciate you all so much. I also want to acknowledge these five amazing people: Marci, Jessie, Brandon, Shernelle, and Farida. Thank you for always supporting me in everything I do. I am so grateful for your love and support.

To my JMotivates community, thank you for rocking with me for all these years. I love that I can encourage you to follow your dreams every single day. You motivate me to keep going. Shout out to these phenomenal Queens: Phebe Jones, Dayna Caddell, Keyondra Lockett, Phyllis Caddell, Jokia, Sidibe, Danielle Stephens McMillian, and Blair Monique. You have showered me with your love and support from the very beginning. I am forever grateful and inspired by you.

To Ms. Katrina, you believed in me since day one! Even in those moments when I started to doubt myself, you were right there reminding me of how amazing I am and poured into my heart with your powerful words of wisdom. You are so special to me. Thank you for your love and support, always.

To Adina, Vincent, Jabril, and Tiffany, I am so glad that God allowed our paths to cross! You have empowered, supported, inspired, and encouraged me to push beyond my limits. You are constantly helping me see that I am stronger than I might realize and to always understand that the small steps of progress count too!

To every mentor, teacher, doctor, and *everyone* who has ever said anything positive or taught me a valuable lesson while on my journey. Thank you all so very much. It means the absolute world to me, and I'll never forget it.

And lastly to my #1 girl in the world, my baby, Sassy, thank you for your love, snuggles, for never judging me, filling me with happiness, and for staying up with me as I worked hard to bring this book to life. I love you with my whole heart.

CHAPTER 1

Ready, Set, Take a Step

Sometimes you have to push yourself out of your comfort zone. For me that often meant mentally and physically. Throughout my childhood, physical therapy encouraged and challenged me to go beyond my limits. I began therapy at the age of four to help strengthen my muscles, increase flexibility and mobility, as well as improve my balance. Gradually, it became a very important part of my daily life.

Therapy was also incorporated into my school schedule. It typically involved taking a few classes in the morning, followed by a session, and concluding the day with a final class before heading home. After the bus dropped me off at home, I would grab a bite to eat and my mom drove me to another therapy clinic for an additional two-hours. Yet, music was what always made my experience more enjoyable. I loved to listen to Selena. A *lot* of Selena! From "Bidi Bidi Bom Bom" to "Where Did the

Feeling Go?", her songs set the tone for my entire workout. By the time I returned home, I'd start my homework. After I was finished, it was time to go to bed and start all over again the next morning. You can imagine I had some hectic days. But it was worth it. For those of you wondering why it was so imperative for me to exercise, let me break it down a bit further.

I have spastic cerebral palsy. This is the most common form of CP where my muscles become tight. The muscle stiffness (spasticity) affects both my arms and legs. Some days my muscles feel loose, but it depends on the day. I can also walk with assistance, but I mainly use my wheelchair to get from place to place. Physical therapy made me feel invincible and instilled in me the importance of determination, courage, and self-discipline.

When I was in fourth grade, I remember eagerly anticipating my therapy session while waiting in homeroom. Cindy's presence at the door brought me a sense of joy through her kindness and encouragement. During our weekly hour-long sessions before lunch, she motivated me to work hard and I often wondered what goal I would accomplish. I loved when therapists pushed me because they not only helped me realize how strong I was, but gave me courage. Each session with her was the highlight of my day. Cindy's question, "Are you ready?" was always met with my enthusiasm and a smile. With a simple "OK, let's go," we would make our way to the therapy room, engaging in casual conversation along the deserted hallways. Once we got there, Cindy would prepare the space, prompting me to unfasten my seatbelt and remove my footplates so she could assist me in transferring onto the mat table. While lying on my back, she started stretching my hamstrings. Due to being in my wheelchair all day, my hamstrings tend to get very tight, and it is difficult to straighten my legs when standing or walking. Placing my leg on her shoulder and gently applying pressure on my knee with her hand, she aimed to lessen the tightness in my hamstring muscles. Believe me, I definitely felt the intensity of the stretch! I have always found stretching to be incredibly beneficial as it helped me stand up straighter and move my legs easier.

I had been making excellent progress in therapy. I used my walker to walk as far as I could down the hallway, which gave Cindy an idea. She told me that she wanted me to walk around the entire school building with my walker. I was terrified. I did not think that I could do it, but somehow, I still wanted to try. I wanted to see how far I could go. Then, Cindy made it even more interesting. She said, "If you walk around the whole school building, I'll buy you Burger King for lunch." I mean, what little girl wouldn't smile about that?

I want to pause for a second and ask you some questions. When was the last time you pushed yourself to see how far you could go? What incentive encouraged you to aspire higher? How did you feel? When Cindy first challenged me, I was very hesitant. I never did anything to this extreme before. What if I failed? Would she still be proud of me? Am I qualified to complete the task? The moment she offered to buy me Burger King, my whole perspective changed. I was ready. I set my mind on the goal, and I was going to try my hardest to reach the finish line.

Fast forward to the following week, it was a bright, sunny

day. The trees were swaying back and forth in the wind, and I was about to do something I had never done. Once Cindy and I were outside, she placed the walker in front of me and wrapped the gait belt around my waist for safety. She helped me out of my wheelchair into the walker, and when I felt secure, we started walking together. Periodically, I stopped to take breaks and catch my breath. Cindy often asked me if I was OK, and, of course, I'd say yes. But the truth is, I started having doubts. I wondered if I had the strength to endure.

Then God stepped in. I realized that if I wanted to complete the goal, I would have to put all my trust in Him. Do you recollect a specific time in your life when you asked God for help? Where were you? What were you doing? How old were you? When situations become hard and overwhelming, the first thing we want to do is quit. We feel like we don't have enough energy to prevail, but that's not true. God will give us what we need, but we must be willing to ask Him for help.

That's what I intended to do. I wanted God to set aside my doubts and help me through the situation. Every time I took a step, God gave me the willpower to carry on. Although I felt my body getting tired, I didn't give up. When I saw my wheelchair, I knew that I was getting closer to the end. Cindy said, "You're almost there. All you have to do is take a couple more steps." I took three more steps 1 … 2 … 3 … and I finally reached my wheelchair. My mission was complete.

Despite feeling exhausted, I was so overjoyed and super proud of myself. Cindy was excited for me as well. Once we were all settled, she asked me for my Burger King order. I wanted a

Whooper, fries, and a Pepsi. Next week, while I was talking to my best friend during lunch, she kept her promise. My face lit up when I saw her, and she said, "Good job! You deserve it."

What I have learned is that you will have to encounter many obstacles to become stronger. At first, I didn't believe it was possible to achieve such a massive goal. Once I let go of my fears, I was able to do far more than I've ever imagined. Now I can do way more than I think I can. You can too. But you must be willing to take the first step.

It is also important to note that sometimes we are not prepared to move forward. That's when God puts our faith to the test. He wants to see if we understand just how strong we really are and if we truly believe it for ourselves. The moment we start believing in ourselves, everything begins to fall into place, and we can focus our attention on how we will reach our ultimate goal. Aren't you glad that you never gave up on yourself? I am because I would have never known the magnitude of my greatness. Speaking of perseverance, I am often reminded of Christina Bell's song "Levels." She informs us that if we want to reap the benefits of what God has in store for our lives, we must keep moving forward. So, I encourage you to step out on faith and accomplish those goals that you've been avoiding out of fear. You just might surprise yourself and discover a strength you never knew you had.

God's Grace Kept Me Playlist

If you are struggling with taking that next step, I have a few songs in mind that will motivate you to do so.

- o "Are You Ready" by Mary Mary
- o "Try" by Keyondra Lockett
- o "Step by Step" by Whitney Houston
- o "It's Like Air" by Sunny Hawkins

CHAPTER 2

When Someone Tells You No

Every now and then, you will encounter people who will
not believe in your dreams. When individuals tried to put
limitations on me, it motivated me to work harder and go after
what I wanted.

A lot has happened since the fourth grade. I underwent
hamstring lengthening surgery, graduated middle school, and
matured into a strong and intelligent teenager who was adjusting
to high school. I loved all my classes but especially English. My
passion for writing began when I was about seven or eight years
old. I'd sit at my parents' kitchen table and just write fictional
stories or dialogues from my favorite television shows like Moesha
and Sister, Sister. Next to the kitchen table was a tall wooden
storage cabinet with drawers where I stashed all my writings.
Sometimes while in class, I would write down lyrics to my favorite
songs, and my friends assumed I wrote them. At the time, I loved

The Diary of Alicia Keys album. "Karma," "Heartburn," "Dragon Days," and "So Simple" were always on repeat. As I got older, my desire for writing only grew stronger. It was just something so calming about pressing my pencil against the paper and allowing my creativity to emerge. I was enjoying every bit of my English class until everything changed.

I was fifteen years old sitting in my freshman English class when my teacher, Mrs. Peterson explained that we would be working on a project about ourselves. She followed it up with two very important questions. "Where do you see yourself in ten years?" "If you could a pick a title to describe your life, what would it be?" I wasn't too happy about doing this project because every time someone asked me the first question, I didn't know what to say. Honestly, I've always been a person who is better at focusing on short-term goals than long-term goals. I was also very shy and disliked talking about myself, so this was going to be a challenge.

As I sat there in the front of the class with my piece of paper and mechanical pencil, I could not think of a title that best described my life. My mind kept drawing a blank. I knew that I wanted to make a powerful statement—a statement that would help people understand me a bit better. To my surprise, I was just about to find out how some of my classmates felt about me. About ten more minutes were left in class when I looked up at the clock on the brick wall. Two male classmates were having a conversation behind me about the project and what career they saw themselves doing in the future. I turned around, smiling because I liked what they were saying about their careers. One of them asked me, "Jennifer, what do you want to do?" I replied, "I want to be a singer." He said, "Oh. That's cool." Before I could say anything, the classmate sitting next to him looked at me with a blank face and then back at him and said, "She can't do that." I initially assumed that he was joking but after studying his facial expression, I quickly realized that he was very serious. Is that how you really feel? What else are you holding back that you aren't telling me?

Has this ever happened to you? I bet some of you could relate to what I'm talking about. Imagine that you just revealed your plans to someone who you thought would be happy for you and being disappointed. Yeah, it isn't a great feeling, right? That's why I didn't say a word. Then, the other classmate looked at him and replied, "She can do whatever she wants to do." When he stood up for me, I felt thankful because he saw more than just my wheelchair.

During the rest of the day, I was trying to process what he said to me. Being a singer was all I ever dreamed about since I was in third grade. I had so many questions. Why would he try to crush my dreams? If I wasn't in a wheelchair, would he have felt the same way? Why wasn't he showing support like the other classmate? Oh, I get it. He's probably never seen a singer in a wheelchair before, but that doesn't mean it's not possible.

After replaying the conversation repeatedly in my head, I decided to not waste my time worrying about the comment that he made. He doesn't define me. If God gave me the desire to be a singer, then neither my classmate nor anybody else can change it. Out of the blue, it dawned on me that I still had not chosen a title for my project. I had recently been listening to a song by Keyshia

Cole called, "Just Like You." Here, she sings about getting to know the real me. How we all have dreams and want to be happy, although each of us has a different vision for our life. It made me remember her. I said, "This is the perfect title for my project."

After putting on the finishing touches, I went to class the next day with a lot of confidence. Mrs. Peterson went around the room and asked each of us the name of our projects. She asked me, "Jennifer, what name did you choose for your project?" I answered with a bright smile, "Just Like You." She smiled back and responded, "I like it," and I knew that I made the right choice.

I've learned a lot of discoveries from this chapter. First, we have already established that some people won't support you and some will. But the most important thing is to believe in yourself. Second, surround yourself with the people who affirm your possibilities and potential. Third, utilize the gifts that God has given you. Fourth, maintain a positive attitude. And fifth, focus on what makes you happy.

I also want you to understand that although I might not be singing professionally, God has given me the opportunity to impart my knowledge to others in another capacity. What I mean is that sometimes we think that we have found our purpose, but God has planned something even greater for our lives. I am grateful that I can combine my passion for writing and music to bring joy to others' hearts. Maybe someday, God might give me the desire to record a song. Who knows? But for now, my focus is motivating you and making sure you don't lose sight of your dreams.

So, if you have a dream, don't let anyone tell you that you can't achieve it. It doesn't matter if you have a disability or have faced many obstacles. You are entitled to pursue your goals like everyone else. I want you to see that when someone tries to discourage you and tell you that you can't accomplish a dream, you must decide whether to believe them.

 God's Grace Kept Me Playlist

Are you still having difficulty finding the strength to believe in your dreams? Well, you're in luck! Here are a couple of songs that will help build your self-esteem and give you the courage to follow your heart. Once you listen to these powerful anthems, you will be reminded that your greatness has no boundaries.

- o "Mirror" by Lalah Hathaway
- o "Hold My Hand" by MAJOR
- o "Just Me" by Danni Baylor
- o "You Are Enough" by Sheléa

CHAPTER 3

It Is Time to Strengthen Your Faith

One of my favorite scriptures in the Bible is "I can do all things through Christ which strengtheneth me" (Philippians 4:13 King James Version). Oftentimes when we go through difficult seasons in our lives, we might find ourselves relying on our faith to bring us out of a situation. Being a Christian woman and having a relationship with God, I know this feeling all too well, and so did my granddad, Tommie Williams. When I think about him and all that he meant to me and my family, I am just in awe. He was such a strong and incredible man who was always so sweet and humble toward everyone that he met. He enjoyed listening to gospel music, but more importantly, he exercised his faith and loved Jesus with all his heart. My granddad read his Bible faithfully, prayed every day, and attended church every Sunday.

When I was younger, my family and I would go to my grandparents' house after church on Sundays. We would laugh and eat dinner together in the dining room. My gram cooked mac and cheese, yams, greens, dressing, ham or chicken, and cornbread. For dessert, she often whipped up her famous sweet potato pie or peach cobbler. I wanted my mom to give me more crust than peaches. The crust was the best part! Then I'd always ask my gram, "Where's Granddad at?" She replied, "He's at church. He should be here in a minute." Sure enough, not even two minutes later, there he was, coming through the back door and into the kitchen. He was dressed in a black suit, holding his black hat with a red feather on the side and carrying his Bible. My granddad walked into the dining room and greeted everyone with a hug while my gram fixed him a plate. He ate a little bit, then he went back to church. Sometimes he wouldn't have time to eat, but he always set aside time to come home and say hello—even if it was just for a few minutes—and then back to church he'd go.

I always say that my granddad was the glue that held everything together. Even when his health began to decline in 2006, my granddad continued to push through. I was thirteen at the time, but I noticed a couple of distinctive factors about him: (1) he never complained, (2) his faith never wavered. When doctors had to amputate both of his legs about a year apart from each other, and he started using a motorized wheelchair, he was a true soldier in my eyes. He did not allow those obstacles to stop him from living his life. Most of all, he kept smiling.

To top it all off, he went to dialysis three times a week. He got up at 5:30 a.m., even during the winter months, and waited outside for the bus to pick him up. I know, it's a lot! But my granddad did what he had to do. I'm pretty sure that most days he was tired or in pain, but I never heard him say those words. Every time I'd ask him, "Are you tired, Granddad?" He responded while shaking his head, "Uh-uh" but I could sense and see the exhaustion on his face. He was just so determined to live and be present for his family.

I always felt like my granddad and I had a very special bond, and it became even stronger as he endured many challenges with his health. It was as if we could both relate and understand each other on a deeper level. I began to reminisce about my experience when he had a therapy session, and I saw him walk with a walker in his prosthetics for the first time. I sat in the dining room as the therapist wrapped the gait belt around his waist and helped him stand. He walked a short distance, but nevertheless I was extremely proud of him. I knew how much energy and strength it took for him to stand and take a few steps. Can you say déjà-vu? I immediately started having flashbacks about my own therapy moments and how I kept going when I didn't feel like I had the strength. I admired him even more.

My granddad often found time to encourage me as well. One Sunday I did not bring my wheelchair inside their house; instead, I walked in with assistance from my mom. As we all came through the front door, I looked straight ahead and saw him sitting in his wheelchair smiling. It's like he had been anticipating for us to come all day. His face was all I needed to see. I went up and gave him the biggest hug. In return, he squeezed me back so tight. My mom went into the kitchen to see my gram. He was wearing a light pink shirt, and I placed both hands on his shoulders so I could hold myself up. All of a sudden, I felt like I was going to lose my balance. He grabbed me gently and said, "I won't let you fall. Hold on to me." He repeated it until he felt like I trusted him and kept his promise. My granddad wanted me to release all my fears and believe that he wasn't going to let me fall.

I can't help but think that God does the same thing when we are tussling to keep our faith afloat. He often reassures us that everything will be fine and encourages us to take His hand. Did you ever have to rely on God to bring you out of a storm? Maybe you felt that God wasn't listening to your prayers, and then He showed up right when you were about to break. I've been there, too. Sometimes we must relinquish everything to God so that He can guide and provide us with what we need to handle the situation. Trust me, I know we might feel afraid at first. But once we surrender, God will begin to work on our behalf. Although we don't see God reaching for our hand, we trust that we will be taken care of by Him. That's what we call faith, and it's what I discovered through that precious moment with my granddad. He also showed me that faith is very powerful. If I want God to do something, I must believe and put my trust in Him. He passed away in 2009, and I still believe that he held on to his faith until the very end. He demonstrated that when you put your faith in God, you don't have to worry because He will strengthen you and bring peace into your life.

My granddad was not only an amazing man who lived for Jesus, but he also taught me some wonderful lessons along the way. I learned about the importance of family. When my granddad would be surrounded by his wife, children, and grandchildren at the dinner table on Sundays, he was so happy. He enjoyed spending quality time with the people who mattered most. I feel that the love he had for his family gave him a reason to keep living even as his health worsened.

He also taught me that there is no point in complaining. Let God fight your battles. My granddad displayed such strength and determination. Those moments when he may have felt like he wanted to give up, he didn't. He continued to push no matter the circumstances.

Additionally, he showed me the significance of encouraging others. Whenever I was in his presence, he always took a minute to embolden my heart. I felt my granddad knew that I doubted myself out of fear and needed an extra push. He desired for me to see what he saw—my strength. He encouraged me to not be afraid and take a chance, which led to him helping me exercise my faith. To this day, I carry all these lessons with me and will cherish them forever.

In what ways are you strengthening your faith with God? All too often, we say that we trust and believe in Him, but when we are put to the test, our minds become absorbed with fear and doubt. God is telling us he is with us, and there is no need to be afraid. But if you want everything to work accordingly, you must complete a few steps first.

* Put your trust in Him.
* Believe He has your best interest at heart.
* Pray. He needs you to talk to Him.
* Read His Word.
* Sing His Praises.
* Tell those around you about Him.

So, are you ready to start strengthening your faith? I encourage you today that whenever you feel defeated, follow these simple steps. You will start to see God working out situations in your life. My granddad had many VCR tapes of *The Canton Spirituals* when I was growing up. One of the songs that I loved listening to was "Glad I Got Jesus." They sing about the beauty of knowing that Jesus will always be there whenever you need Him. All you must do is believe, and He will take care of everything else.

 God's Grace Kept Me Playlist

Do you currently feel that your faith is not strong enough and would like to strengthen it? I highly recommend that you listen to the songs below to increase your faith and take you to the next level with God.

- o "Nobody Like You Lord" by Maranda Curtis
- o "I'll Just Say Yes" by Brian Courtney Wilson
- o "In the Midst of It All" by Yolanda Adams
- o "This Is A Move (Live)" by Tasha Cobbs Leonard

CHAPTER 4

No Matter What Happens in Life, Never Give Up

L ife is a quest. Sometimes you will stumble upon many speed bumps and get lost before you reach your destination. It isn't always perfect or what we planned, but we get an opportunity to learn something new. When we don't understand why, there's always a powerful message that follows. Whenever I was stuck at a crossroad, God placed certain people in my life to remind me to never give up on my dreams.

It was August 2009, and I just started my sophomore year of high school. I was still dealing with losing my granddad a month earlier but was excited to see friends and optimistic about what this school year would bring. I entered the building, rocking my Dereon jeans, and a new hairstyle—styled in a bob with bangs because I wanted something different.

I was always nervous during the first day of school because

I had to familiarize myself with the atmosphere again. Not only that, but I genuinely looked forward to meeting my new teachers every year. It was vitally important to me that they exemplified kindness and offered unwavering support so I could become the best version of myself.

As the day went on, I was anxious to get to English class. I arrived a couple minutes early so that I could find the perfect seat. A few other students were trying to find seats as well. The teacher wasn't there yet, but I wanted to be prepared for when she entered the classroom. I opened my notebook and grabbed a pencil out of my case so that I could take notes. Suddenly, I saw a woman gliding gracefully in her wheelchair through the hallway, approaching the classroom. She came through the door with the biggest smile and noticed me immediately. It only took a few seconds for me to realize that she was my teacher. I was also surprised to learn that she used a wheelchair too.

I couldn't believe that it was happening. No one knew, but I often dreamed of this day. I imagined having a teacher who looked like me and understood my daily struggles. Have you ever dreamt of something, and it became a reality? Well, this was my life. Up until this point, I never had a teacher who navigated life from a wheelchair. This was my first experience.

Once class began, she went in front of the classroom and introduced herself to all of us. "Hi, I'm Mrs. Wayne." Then she said very bluntly, "Oh, before we get started, how many of you know why I am in a wheelchair?"

The moment she asked that question, she caught me off guard a bit. I didn't think she was going to say anything about it, but she did the exact opposite. She told us that when she was in high school, she was in a car accident. I believe that Mrs. Wayne wanted to be open and honest with her students. She understood that people would be curious and didn't want to leave room for any whispers or misconceptions. She explained what happened and moved on. She spoke her truth and didn't sugarcoat it. I admired her for that because she didn't have to tell us anything. In that moment, I knew that I was supposed to be in Mrs. Wayne's class.

In many ways, I felt like Mrs. Wayne understood me. Not just because she used a wheelchair and we both shared the love of writing, but she showed me what is possible and that my dreams should never be put on hold because of my disability. I can have the life I want. Of course, she dealt with the constant stares when out in public and had to ask people for help, but she was not going to stop living her life because her circumstances changed. She desired to live every day to the fullest. Even through her teaching, she wanted everyone to apply themselves and believe in their full potential. Whether we were writing an essay, learning new vocabulary words, or reading a novel, that's what she expected. If you were trying your best, she would encourage you. When you were struggling, she'd help you understand the material. Sometimes she would make us do the work on our own to see how much effort and time we would put into the assignment. Then we all discussed it during our next class meeting.

There was one core memory that stood out to me. It was when Mrs. Wayne taught us how to write a five-paragraph essay with a prompt. We had to decide whether students should wear uniforms and provide three reasons to support our claim. Once I finished writing, I turned it in for grading. By the next class, I found out that I received an A on my essay. I put my work in my folder and was getting ready to leave when she stopped me. She said that she wanted to use my essay as an example for the other students to follow. "I'll give it back to you tomorrow," she said. I was not only proud of myself but honored that she used my paper to help my classmates. Mrs. Wayne noticed my work ethic, my determination, my positive attitude, and passion for writing. She mainly wanted to make sure that I believed in myself as much as she did. She continued to support me all the way to the end of the school year, and that's what I had hoped for since the beginning. I know that God did this. He placed her in my life for a reason, and not only did she teach my favorite subject, but she was kind, and everyone adored her. She was my English teacher until I completed high school.

Furthermore, Mrs. Wayne poured a lot of wisdom into me, and I've learned several poignant lessons from her. She modeled how to own my truth and tell my story unapologetically. She taught me to be kind and encourage others. She showed me by example that there are no limits when it comes to my disability. She influenced me to always believe in my potential. She also demonstrated that when you are diligent, your efforts should be celebrated. I discovered through Mrs. Wayne that helping others can boost one's confidence and propel them further toward their dreams. She proved that dreams are endless, and I can create the life I want. Lastly, she taught me that no matter what happens in life, never give up.

There will be moments in your life when certain obstacles will try to defeat you, but I want to let you know that you will win. Even if you feel like you do not have the strength, God will give it to you. In Yolanda Adams's song "Never Give Up," she encourages us to keep trying. Life isn't always easy, and we will go through a whirlwind of emotions, but that doesn't mean we quit. We take every setback and use it as ammunition to push forward. I also want to add that it is vitally important to surround yourself with people who will help you prosper and succeed. They just might provide you with essential tools that lead you to your destiny.

 God's Grace Kept Me Playlist

It can be very difficult when you are trying so hard to accomplish something, but you keep encountering hurdles. You become defeated because you feel like you are not making any progress. Whenever I contemplated giving up, I'd listen to these songs, and they reminded that the best is yet to come! I encourage you to do the same.

- o "Unfinished" by Mandisa
- o "Depending On You" by Gene Moore
- o "I Didn't Know My Own Strength" by Whitney Houston
- o "I'm Alive" by Celine Dion

CHAPTER 5

Appreciate the Small Things

W hen was the last time you stopped to reflect on the many blessings that you have received? Just let that sink in for a moment. Maybe it was this morning, last week, a couple of months ago, or you probably can't even remember. A lot of times, we get so caught up in our own busyness that we forget to recognize them or unintentionally take everything for granted. I was always told to appreciate what I have because life can change in the blink of an eye.

Here's another realistic truth. All too often, we concentrate on what we want instead of what we've already been given. Then we end up missing an important message that offers us a broader perspective about life itself. We also don't know what our future holds, which is why we need to cherish every second and be grateful for what we are blessed with. A crucial moment in my life made me realize every gift has a meaning. We might not understand the significance right away, but it can have a tremendous impact on you.

I was seventeen, and it was the last day of my junior year in high school. A few days earlier, I had visited the doctor who told me that I needed adductor surgery over the summer. Due to muscle tightness caused by spasticity, my legs would sometimes cross over each other when walking. This is known as scissoring. My doctor felt that surgery was the best option to fix the problem. By lengthening my inner thigh muscles, I would be able to walk better. He said, "You'll have the surgery, recuperate at home for twelve days, then I want to send you to rehab immediately." I was nervous, but God gave me a sign to let me know that everything was going to be OK.

The night before my surgery, I was lying in bed skimming through Music Choice On Demand and stumbled upon a live concert series by the Gospel duo Mary Mary. I became a fan of their music in 2000 when they debuted their first single, "Shackles" (Praise You), and every time I heard Erica and Tina sing, they brought such happiness into my heart. As I scrolled down the list of songs on my TV, I saw the title "I Worship You" and desired to check it out. It was from their fifth studio album, *The Sound*, which was released in 2008. When I pressed play, there was no way I could've predicted what would happen next.

The second I heard the lyrics "You took everything I was, made me what I am. And with all I am I worship you," I immediately fell in love with the song and its message. It's as if God led me there—to comfort me, calm my fears, and ultimately replenish my faith. With my eyes closed and tears streaming down my face, I experienced an indescribable connection with God that I didn't even know I needed. I ended up listening to that song until the wee hours of the morning. The next day on the way to the hospital, I still had the song on repeat. I just couldn't shake that moment with God. These words ignited something in my soul. Unbeknownst to me, God wasn't done yet.

I never told anyone this, but when I woke up in the recovery room, still groggy from anesthesia and in pain, I felt God's presence heavily surrounding me. Right then, my life changed. I'd experienced His presence in the past, but never of this magnitude. This time was unlike the rest. For those of you who want to know what God's presence feels like, I'll paint a vivid picture for you. It reminded me of a hug—a tight, gentle squeeze intertwined with love, warmth, and encouragement. His tender embrace lifted my spirit and gave me strength. I felt stronger and more determined than I ever have in my entire life. Once you've gone through a moment like this with God, you won't ever be the same, and it's definitely something you'll never forget. If you are someone who knows what it feels like to be in the presence of God, I encourage you to hold onto those moments and keep them as a daily reminder of how good God has been to you. He will always be right there no matter the circumstances. I couldn't quite understand the essence of what God was trying to say. But I'd soon find out what this moment meant and why.

While recovering at home for about two weeks, I started picturing rehab and the goals that I hoped to accomplish. I mainly wanted to strengthen my legs and improve my endurance so that

I could walk longer distances. I would like to take a minute to talk about the importance of setting goals. First, I have a couple of questions for you. How do you define success? Do you see yourself achieving more, but you don't know where to start? Well, you can begin by setting some goals. You can either write them down on paper, speak them into the atmosphere, create a vision board, or simply tape them on your bedroom wall. The purpose of setting goals for ourselves is to help us stay focused and motivated. Sometimes we can become easily distracted and lose sight of what we came to accomplish. But when goals are put in place, we can keep track of our progress and reach our greatest potential. We also must construct a plan on how we can achieve them. When that's completed, we will be on the right path and equipped for success. Every time I set a goal, I was clear about my intentions and ready to put in the work. I envisioned myself conquering the goal and realized that I'd have to keep pushing until I reached a place of satisfaction.

Upon entering the rehabilitation center, I observed numerous individuals utilizing wheelchairs, walkers, crutches, and other mobility aids. We might have been on our own individual journeys, but one thing we had in common was that we all desired to become stronger. My doctor, who also a wheelchair user, was not only incredibly kind and welcoming, but she also exuded a sense of understanding and empathy that immediately put my mind at ease. After she evaluated me and checked to make sure that my scars were healing properly, she told me to get some rest because I started therapy the next day.

A few weeks later, I found out that my roommate had to be

transported somewhere else, and another person was going to take her place. The next day after finishing my therapy session, I was watching *All My Children*, and the paramedics wheeled someone on a stretcher into my room. I immediately thought, *Oh my goodness, this must be my new roommate.* At first, I couldn't really see the person's face. I waited for one of the paramedics to move aside. When she was transferred from the stretcher to the bed, I was not prepared for what I was about to see.

My new roommate was a limb loss warrior and survivor. Bailey truly embodied the essence of strength and resilience. She excelled in various activities, showing dedication in her studies, and exuding a positive energy in every room she entered. Bailey also experienced a significant turning point within her journey - a life-saving amputation. This event marked a new chapter for Bailey, requiring her to relearn essential daily tasks like feeding herself and brushing her teeth. Though Bailey endured many obstacles, she continued to power through, her spirit remained strong, and her light always shined bright.

One night when we were both in bed, a nurse came into the room to check on her. My curtain was slightly open, and I could see everything that was going on. When the nurse saw Bailey for the first time, she immediately began to cry and left abruptly. After a few seconds, she came back and said, "I'm sorry" with tears streaming down her face. The nurse further explained that she didn't usually work on this floor, and the situation caught her by surprise. Amid the nurse pulling herself together, Bailey started rubbing the nurse's back and consoling her by saying "Don't cry.

It's going to be OK." She wasn't even worried about herself; she only cared about the well-being of the nurse.

Meanwhile, I was behind my curtain crying too. I could not believe how much resilience she had. She could've wept alongside the nurse or dwelled on her current situation, but that didn't happen. Instead, she mustered up the courage in the wake of her traumatic experience to comfort others and remain calm. After the nurse exited the room, I dried my tears and began to pray. I asked God to bless Bailey and let her know that she was not alone, and everything will work out. The next morning, I knew that God heard my prayers. Bailey got fitted for her prosthesis. She began smiling more, and all the therapists were so proud of her progress.

A few months after I left the rehabilitation center, My mom took me to visit Bailey so I could see how she was doing. While we were waiting in the lobby, I looked through the glass window and noticed that she was a pro at feeding herself. What an enormous accomplishment! Suddenly, she came out in her wheelchair alongside the therapist and yelled, "Hey, Jennifer!" A huge smile was on her face, she was so happy. It warmed my heart to see how far she'd come and what wonderful opportunities awaited her in the future. I felt extremely blessed to have crossed paths with her.

As we were getting ready to leave, everything started coming together. I understood exactly what God was doing in that sacred moment with me. I originally thought He was just comforting me after my surgery, but His message was much bigger. God was reminding me of how important it is to worship Him through the good and the bad times. What became even clearer is the simple fact that God didn't have to bring me this far, and because of His graciousness, I must continue to put Him first in everything I do and be grateful. Bailey taught me some powerful lessons, too!

Bailey helped me see life through a different lens She reminded me that I might have a disability, but I am still here doing my very best. It might take me a little bit longer to complete a task, but it eventually gets done. I started focusing on what I can do, instead of what I cannot do. She showed me that sometimes you must put others' needs before your own. Bailey taught me that you can rebuild your life and find peace after a life-altering experience. She also proved that if you keep trying, you will prevail. Listen, I want you to think about your victories and not every defeat. Life is so precious, and if God has allowed you the opportunity to see another day, make each moment count.

Sunny Hawkins's song "Where Would I Be" sums up this powerful story. It is one of my favorites because she sings about the splendor of God's unconditional love and how it transforms our life. She also highlights the importance of being grateful for it all—storms, rainbows, pleasure, and pain. One thing we must hold onto is that everything in our life works together to make us more of who we were created to be. The key is to make up our mind to enjoy the journey by appreciating it all—large and small.

God's Grace Kept Me Playlist

What are you grateful for today? We have all had moments when we wanted more, and we failed to appreciate what we already have. If you ever need a friendly reminder, I suggest you play these songs that I've listed on my playlist.

- o "I Worship You" by Mary Mary
- o "So Grateful" by Dayna Caddell ft. Israel Houghton
- o "My Everything" by Bri Babineaux
- o "Look No Further" by Evvie McKinney

CHAPTER 6

You Are Perfect Just the Way You Are

What do you see when you look at yourself in the mirror? Are you analyzing every flaw or learning how to embrace your beauty? Sometimes we are extremely hypocritical of ourselves, which makes us question who we are as individuals. We desire to be perfect, and when something is out of place, we begin to fall apart at the seams. Like many of us, I often criticized myself. I worried about what others thought about me and didn't always understand my worth. One day I started to accept my imperfections and be comfortable in my own skin.

From sixth to eleventh grade, my best friend Marci and I were inseparable. She was a year older than me, but we did everything together. We rode the same school bus, we sat by each other at lunch, we waited for each other to get out of class, and we even took a class together—forensic science with one of our favorite professors, Ms. G! It made both of us happy that we could see each other every day, but everything changed in 2012. I was eighteen and completing my senior year, but there was one problem. My best friend was not there. Marci graduated a year earlier, and I was all by myself. (Well, at least that's how it felt.) To go from having your friend there with you all the time to not having her at all really was tough. Don't get me wrong, I was elated that she was going to college, and we still talked on the phone, but it just wasn't the same.

I even sat by myself at lunch. You could hear all the commotion of people talking and laughing with their friends, and I would just write in my notebook until lunch was over. It wasn't that nobody wanted to sit with me; I was extremely shy and kept to myself. I was not the girl who would start a random conversation with someone. At times, Mrs. Bowlds would come into the lunchroom and encourage me to socialize with others. She'd sneak up on me and say gently, "Go find someone to sit with." I'd look at her with a convincing smile, but on the inside, I felt like I was drowning. As each day passed, I was sinking deeper and deeper until I was no longer able to hold my head above water. I know that she hated seeing me sit at a table all alone. A part of me wanted to so badly, but I could not do it. I saw classmates and people who I knew that I contemplated sitting by, but I just couldn't move.

What she didn't know was that I was scared. I was afraid of how others would perceive me. Why, you might ask? It is because people have said negative things about me before, and I did not want to go through that again. Many times I thought to myself, *Maybe if I were not in a wheelchair, then it would be so much easier to socialize with people.* I would not have to worry about people staring at me all the time, feeling uncomfortable, or being prejudged before they got the opportunity to even know me.

I never disclosed my feelings to Mrs. Bowlds because I knew that she'd worry. Honestly, this wasn't her battle to fight. I wanted to handle the situation on my own terms. I battled with this issue every day and suffered in silence. One day while writing in my notebook, I heard God whispering to me. He said, "I created you, Jennifer. You were made in my image. There is no need to question who you are." Even though God spoke these words, I still had doubts. I couldn't seem to let go of the negativity. I figured that if I just buried my face into my notebook, everything would eventually disappear. All the noise, the people, and my feelings of loneliness, anxiety, low self-esteem, fear, and sadness would cease. But it didn't. I remained in this headspace for months. Something had to give; I was on the verge of my breaking point.

A few months later, I was introduced me to a new student named Stephanie who was so kind and down-to-earth. I was a little hesitant to open up because I wasn't sure if she'd be receptive to getting to know me. I had built up a wall for so long that I almost missed the opportunity to gain a great friend. So, we started sitting together at lunch. Ah, I could finally breathe again! I felt so relieved. I didn't have to be alone. More importantly, I loved that she never judged me, and she treated me like a real

---

To my beautiful friend Stephanie, I dedicate this chapter with deep gratitude for the light she brought into my life. Her memory and story continue to live on through these pages, serving as a heartfelt tribute to the lasting impact she had on me. Although my original wish was to share this book with her once it was published, I now carry her in my heart forever.

person, which was all I wanted. We instantly became friends, and I learned that she was also battling a few health challenges as well. If she hadn't told me, I would've never known what she was going through. I saw the visible scars on her arms, but she never let her circumstances affect her spirit. She came to school every day, was very sociable, and didn't care what others had to say. Now, she'd speak her mind if necessary, but she stayed true to herself.

So, here I am. I'm sitting with my new friend at lunch, having a great time. You'd think that I'd be the happiest person on earth—nope, not quite. You see, my friend had accepted me for who I was, but I still didn't feel ready. One day while we were getting settled at our usual spot, she yelled across the table trying to get another friend's attention. They spoke briefly, then she went to grab some food to eat. As she walked away, I was amazed that she already made friends, and it had only been a few weeks. I wished that I had the same confidence as my awesome friend. Then, I started reflecting on what God revealed to me months prior and wondered, "How could I ever doubt God?" He's absolutely right. I am smart, kind, hardworking, beautiful, and a wonderful person. There is a reason why God made me this way, and I should be proud of who I am. If my friend can love herself unconditionally, why can't I follow in her footsteps?

When did you discover your own self-worth? Was there an individual or a specific memory that led you in that direction? Sometimes when God speaks to us, we are unable to see our unique qualities because we lack confidence and belief in ourselves. We feel compelled to change who we are and try to hide from the rest of the world, hoping that it will eventually make us whole again. Unfortunately, that doesn't work. The reality is that if we stick with a negative mindset and avoid our feelings, we are only making the situation more difficult. For us to be in a position to receive God's messages and rebuild our self-esteem, we need to be honest with what we want and peel back the layers until we get to the root of the problem. We must also be willing to let others in. It took me a while to realize that what I had been doing wasn't healthy. I had to dig deep within myself and find my happiness. I truly believe with some self-care and reevaluating, you can uncover yours as well.

While rediscovering myself, I found out that Stephanie and I had a lot more in common than I realized. Every day until we graduated, we laughed and enjoyed each other's company. Here are some key lessons that I want you to absorb.

* You don't need other people to validate you.
* Never feel pressured to change for anyone.
* God affirms our worth, but we must see it for ourselves before we can start feeling better.
* Trust the process and understand that change won't happen overnight.
* Speak positive affirmations to yourself daily.
* Consider doing some soul searching to find your inner happiness.
* Be open to new friends.
* We must put ourselves out there and accept new friendships.

As this story comes to an end, I find myself meditating on the lyrics to Colbie Caillat's song "Try." She uses her voice to encourage us to love ourselves unconditionally. We have all tried or felt pressured to live up to other people's expectations, but we must understand that we can't please everyone. The most important thing that we can do is realize that our happiness comes first.

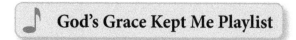

God's Grace Kept Me Playlist

A few years ago, I was having a conversation with my wonderful friend Donna, and she gave me some great advice that I want to share with you. She said, "Jennifer, stop hiding. Come out from behind the scenes." These words moved me in more ways than one and I never forgot them. At times, I still revert to this message when I'm feeling insecure. If you're dealing with low self-esteem or isolating yourself from others, please know that you are valuable, and you will always be perfect in God's eyes. I also would like for you to take a moment to listen to these songs. After you're finished, you will feel rejuvenated and slowly start to uncover the magic that lives inside of you.

- o "Stop And Stare" by Angelina Sherie
- o I'm a Fan" by Erica Campbell
- o "Amazing" by Latice Crawford
- o "Take Me As I Am" by Zie'l

CHAPTER 7

God Chose Me

I believe in my heart that each of us was chosen, which simply means God handpicked all of us to fulfill a specific purpose on earth. We might not always understand His plan or why we feel drawn to go in a particular direction, but what remains true is that we must take His request and be prepared to put it into action. By setting the plan in motion, we're able to serve others and give God the glory. Initially, I was completely unaware of what God wanted from me. I had no idea that once I found my path, God would open the doors to endless possibilities and opportunities and help me see my own potential.

Ever since I was a little girl, I often wondered why God chose me. I remember when I was six years old, trying to climb into my parents' rocking chair all by myself. It was dark brown, sitting between the couch and treadmill in the basement. I'd never sat in one before, and I loved that the chair swayed back and forth. I just desired to have some fun. My mom offered to help me, but I wanted to see if I could do it on my own. While on the floor, I got on my knees and tried to pull myself up. I was unsuccessful the first time. So, I tried again. The rocking chair kept moving on me.

With every ounce of strength, I kept trying over and over. After several attempts, I became frustrated. I fell back on my knees and started crying, screaming at the top of my lungs, "*Why? Why? Why?*" I wondered why certain tasks were difficult for me but easy for others? Why did I have to be born with cerebral palsy? Why am I in a wheelchair? How would my life be different if I didn't have a disability? Do you recall a moment in your life when you just cried out to God? What happened after you released those emotions? Sometimes we must learn to give ourselves permission to let the tears flow and understand that it's OK to cry. We cannot keep everything bottled up, nor can we stay in that low place. After about twenty minutes, I wiped my eyes and began to calm down.

As I got older, those questions still plagued my mind. When I would hear and read stories about people who were born prematurely and walking on their own, I wanted that life. I just wished I could trade places to see how it felt to do things without accommodations such as getting in the car to get something to eat, not having to search for accessible seating at a concert, or enlisting the help of a family member because there is no ramp connected to the building. One evening while sitting in my room with my door closed, I asked God a question. I asked Him, "God what is your purpose for my life?" I was so confused and needed clarity. Little did I know that He was about to reveal the answer in a major way.

I was attending Sunday school at my childhood church, where I first started singing the choir and where my dad baptized my sisters, Jan, Jess, and me. The water was so cold that I cried. Back then, my grandma Rosie was our teacher, and she conducted our classes in the prayer room. This room provided a cozy and intimate setting where she, along with other missionaries, would come together after the morning worship to connect with God and pray for others.

The prayer room usually stayed locked, so my grandma used a key to get inside. A few chairs were lined up against the wall, which had a picture of the Last Supper. Some Sundays, I'd have difficulty maneuvering my wheelchair because of the narrow space, but my sisters always took care of me.

I am the middle child. There is a two-year gap between me and Jess. Jan and I are only ten months apart—she's my Irish twin! Not to mention, all our names begin with J so you can just about imagine the confusion when people saw us. We were raised in a loving, supportive faith-based home in the south suburbs of Chicago where our parents instilled in us three main principles: pursue an education, have a relationship with God, and always remain humble. We went to church twice a week.

On Friday nights, we had choir rehearsal and wore blue jean skirts with different color tops. We'd practice for about an hour, then my mom would take us to Gram's house to eat fried catfish. Mmmm, the food smelled so delicious coming from the kitchen. Then we got up early on Sunday morning and even stayed if there was an afternoon service. I was twelve when we became PKs (preacher's kids) as my dad joined the ministry. We genuinely enjoyed watching him preach because he was so knowledgeable about God's word. His sermons were very thought-provoking. He'd break down each story piece by piece, implementing realistic illustrations to help us understand the power behind the message. When he finished, you'd leave the sanctuary uplifted and begin to examine your own life choices.

Music was also an enormous part of our lives. We listened to everything from Teddy Pendergrass to Natalie Cole to Shirley Caesar. My dad often went in the basement and blasted all his gospel records—the music was so loud that you could feel the vibration through the floor. We relied on music whenever there was a storm, and the lights went out. We'd gather in the kitchen, and he would teach us songs from his favorite quartet groups or music that he wrote during his younger days.

Jess sang soprano, Jan held down alto, and I sang tenor. (I started out singing alto but switched when we began singing together.) We had our share of disagreements—Jess wanted to pick every song and didn't go with any of our suggestions. All she wanted to sing were songs by the Clark Sisters. Jan and I loved the Clark Sisters too, but we also wanted to try new things and expand our horizons. Once we ironed out the kinks, we were magical. Sometimes my mom joined us as well, just for fun. Truthfully, I loved to sing, but I felt that my voice wasn't good enough.

During our rehearsals, I was somewhat discouraged because I could not hit certain notes. When I practiced in my room, the notes came out smoothly. Whenever it was time for me to sing in front of my sisters, I was a ball of nerves. As a result, my voice couldn't produce the clear and precise notes that I had yearned for. Since they sounded perfect already, I refused to hold my sisters back. They eventually started performing on afternoon church programs with my dad, while my mom and I cheered them on from the audience. My sisters pleaded for me to sing, but I always declined their offer. They would say, "We need you, Jenny." I responded, "No, you don't. You're doing fine without me." I didn't want to interfere with their vibe. A few months later, they were asked to perform again. Instead of asking me, my sisters went to my mom to try and convince me. After talking with her, I decided to give it a try. I was nervous, but they were so happy to finally have me sing with them. We ended up performing "Be Grateful," by Walter Hawkins, and received a standing ovation, and the crowd loved us. The spirit of Jesus filled the room, and it was so exhilarating. From that point on, my sisters and I continued to sing for a while and encouraged each other.

One Sunday morning when I was nineteen, my sisters and I were reviewing the lesson while listening to our grandma speak. She always had a way of capturing one's attention with her words. She asked us these important questions. She said, "What is your gift?" "What is it that God has called you to do?" She gave us a moment to think about it. Jan revealed her gift first. Jess wasn't sure of her gift yet. Then my grandma, while standing directly in front of me, asked, "Jennifer, what is your gift?" I looked into her eyes and confidently said, "I believe that I am here to inspire people." At that moment, I felt as if a weight was lifted off my shoulders. God heard me! He really heard me. It was the best feeling in the world. What made me even more excited was that I finally understood the reason for God choosing me. I knew what His purpose was for my life, and I did not take it lightly. I found myself encouraging my friends and those around me.

As if that wasn't reassuring enough, four years later, Latice Crawford released her *EP Diary of a Church Girl*. A song on the project was called "Choose Me." This message reminded me that I've been chosen by God to inspire others, and there is power in my gift. As a child, I was so confused as to why I was born with cerebral palsy and had to use a wheelchair. I thought if I didn't have a disability, my life would be a lot better, or I'd be happier. But God gradually showed me over the years that I had something extraordinary to offer the world. Through singing with my sisters, I was able to touch so many lives with my voice. Although, we don't sing together anymore, God provided me a bigger platform, where I can use music to inspire and motivate others daily. At first, I couldn't see the beauty in God's plan because I only saw a small portion, not the whole picture. I now understand that my gift is part of my divine design, and I can inspire people because I am an overcomer.

So, what has God chosen you for? As you are discovering your path, you might feel stuck or believe that you don't have a purpose, but that's far from the truth. God has bestowed special gifts upon all of us. We weren't brought here by mistake. God intentionally chose us for a reason, but to understand His desires, we must be ready to listen to the message that awaits us. Oftentimes when God speaks, we are hesitant because we want to follow through with our own plans. Then if God is silent, we think we're being forgotten. We must realize that God only wants the best for His people. One way that we can start is to be patient and recognize that although God might not always provide us with an immediate response, He is listening. Isn't it so beautiful to know that God chose you? Whenever we are in doubt, let's take into consideration that we are qualified to complete God's work with the intent of making a lasting impact on others and glorifying His name.

 God's Grace Kept Me Playlist

Are you struggling to find your place and feel discouraged because God hasn't responded to your prayers? While you wait, here's what I want you to do. First, close your eyes and take a deep breath. Second, go grab your air pods or headphones and whatever device you use to listen to music. Finally, check out these songs below. I hope it blesses you!

- o "Overcomer" by Mandisa
- o "Heavenly Father" by Keyondra Lockett
- o "Grace" by Tasha Cobbs Leonard
- o "Something Out of Nothing" by Jessica Reedy

CHAPTER 8

I Am Blossoming into
Something Beautiful

In every season, we experience a shift. Some of those changes
can be wonderful or have you feeling like you are spiraling
out of control. While we are adjusting and wondering why it's
happening, we don't see the incredible transformation that is
about to unfold. Every time I had to face my fears, I was always
so scared and shied away from it all—not knowing that I would
eventually have to break out of my shell, spread my wings, and
fly gracefully like a butterfly.

In the fall of 2013, I was visiting my counselor Mrs. Thompson
to go over my study plan. She was reviewing all the classes I had
taken so far. Then she asked the question that I had been dreading
for the longest time since I started college. "Are you ready to take
speech class yet?" I replied with nervousness in my voice, "No.
Is there any way that I could just skip it?" She laughed and said,

"Nope. You have to take it." Before this appointment, I purposely avoided taking speech for an entire year because I hated public speaking. The moment I would go up to speak in front of people, my heart raced superfast, my whole body became hot, and I felt like I could not breathe. I also wondered when giving a speech, what is the audience thinking? Can they see my hands trembling? Are they really listening to me or just looking at my wheelchair? I just wanted people to see Jennifer, not my disability. After a lot of convincing from Mrs. Thompson, I promised her that I would register for the class as soon as possible. We both smiled, and I left her office scared out of my mind, but who knew that this journey I was about to embark on would change my life forever.

I normally arrived at school around 8:15 a.m. Since Spanish class didn't start until 9:00 a.m., I would go to the computer lab and listen to music. It calmed my spirit and helped me conquer my day. Sometimes I even got a chance to get a head start on my homework assignments, which was a plus. There was a glass window behind the computer, so when I looked at the screen, I could see students in the hallway and professors going back and forth to their offices. One morning while sitting at the computer with my earplugs in, I saw a sophisticated woman walk past the window. She was wearing a blue blazer with gold buttons and black dress pants. She appeared so confident and professional. I said to myself, "I don't know what subject she teaches, but I want her to be my teacher." There was just something about her that caught me by surprise. As the day went by, I never forgot her face. Before I knew it, the spring semester had arrived. It was time for me to face one of my biggest fears. I closed my eyes, took a deep breath, and gave myself a pep talk to boost my confidence. Let's chat for a second. What affirmations did you tell yourself when overcoming your fears? How did it help increase your self-assurance? When having to do something that makes us feel uncomfortable, we often start jumping to conclusions. "I don't think I can handle it." "What if something goes wrong?" "Am I really strong enough for this?" It's normal to second-guess ourselves when faced with a challenge, but we cannot allow situations to get us down. Instead, start speaking highly of yourself. You will see that you have everything you need to rise above any fear that tries to hinder your success. I decided that I wasn't going to let fear win. I put my trust in God and made a vow that I would try my hardest to conquer public speaking.

When I entered the classroom, there she was. It was the same woman I saw through the glass window that I had admired from afar. She was standing by the whiteboard, waiting for class to start. Was I dreaming? It was so surreal. I couldn't believe what I was seeing. She was everything I imagined her to be and more. She smiled, introduced herself to the students, and said, "I'm going to tell you about myself in the form of a story." When she began the narrative, she immediately captured my attention with her sweet personality and warm spirit. As a requirement for the class, each student had to prepare four speeches throughout the semester—narrative, demonstration, informative, and persuasive. In my mind, I was overwhelmed, but Mrs. Page always encouraged me and gave the best advice.

I will never forget her reaction when I presented my informative speech. I chose cerebral palsy as my topic because I wanted to spread awareness about my disability and give others an opportunity to learn more about it. As I started speaking, I could tell out of the corner of my eye that Mrs. Page was listening attentively to what I had to say. I felt as if she wanted me to succeed. I could hear her (in my head) saying, "You can do this, Jennifer." After the speech was over, I exhaled deeply and felt proud of myself that I didn't let my anxiety get the best of me. When everyone completed their speeches, she provided us with tips on how to improve, and what I love most is that she always asked this question: "What are some takeaways that you have learned from your speech?" This was very profound because it showed that Mrs. Page cared deeply about her students and their well-being. She desired to hear her student's thoughts and concerns, which meant the absolute world to me. She also had something special up her sleeve that I didn't even see coming.

While taking my final exam for speech class, I was ecstatic because I conquered a fear that I had been avoiding for so long. It was a nerve-racking experience, but I'm so glad I hung in there! I then raised my hand to let Mrs. Page know that I was finished. She walked over, grabbed my scantron, and handed me an envelope. I thought to myself, *I wonder what's inside.* When I got home, I opened the envelope to find an invitation to a dinner that she was hosting at a restaurant. All I could think about was, "What did I ever do to deserve this invite?" She picked me out of all the people. I felt so grateful. When I arrived at the dinner, twelve women whom she chose from her other classes were sitting at the table, too. While eating and conversing, Mrs. Page began explaining the reason she invited all of us to such a lovely dinner.

It was then that I realized her purpose for wanting me there as well as the other women. She wanted to celebrate our hard work and inspire us to complete our associate's degrees and never give up on our dreams. She also told us that in 2012, God gave her a vision to start an organization.

As if the night could not get any sweeter, she inducted all of us into the organization with framed, personalized certificates. The thing that touched my heart the most is that Mrs. Page saw me. She saw Jennifer and not my disability. She saw something special in me that I honestly did not even see in myself. Mrs. Page gave me strength and reminded me that I can achieve my goals no matter the circumstances. She also gave me confidence, and it is because of her that I met another one of my best friends, Jessie! She has cerebral palsy as well, and she's one of the most generous, caring, and supportive people I've ever had the pleasure of knowing. I believe that she was meant to be in my life, and I'm so thankful for her friendship. More importantly, Mrs. Page showed me that I am blossoming into something beautiful every day. That means with every experience, I am evolving— becoming stronger, wiser, and fearless. I will forever be grateful to her for that powerful lesson. To this day, I am still a part of her organization, and she remains a very influential person in my life. I cherish her deeply.

Are you ready to start blossoming? When facing fears, we might feel it's easier to run and hide. But that only works until we can no longer avoid the situation. We will eventually have to tear down the wall we've built and finally confront our reality. First, we must understand why we chose to flee. In most cases, we are afraid of the unknown. Since we are unable to see what lies ahead, we assume that we're going to fail and let our past experiences define our present. By doing that, we essentially stop our growth. Then, if we want to see a breakthrough, we need to release all those emotions and embrace the strength within us. It's also important that we encourage ourselves daily. While overcoming my fear of public speaking, I'd listen to "Looking Like," by Erica Campbell. She reminded me that in life obstacles will come, but I am strong enough to make it, and you can too. We also must realize that to blossom, we must go through the process with an open mind. Here's what I've learned from my experience:

* Being sensitive to people God places in your path.
* Asking friends to join you on the journey.
* Stepping out of your comfort zone.
* Doing what's required to meet your goals.
* Finding ways to enhance your skills.
* Realizing you are more than your circumstances.
* Trusting the process even when you don't see the results.
* Believing you can conquer anything you set your mind to.
* Confronting your fears helps you discover more about yourself.
* Growing not only makes you stronger but molds you into who you were called to be.

God's Grace Kept Me Playlist

As you evolve, blossom, and step into your purpose, I want you to know that you have what it takes to succeed. If while in the process, you feel overwhelmed or doubt begins to seep into your mind, check out these songs from my playlist and trust that your time is coming!

- o "Speed Racing" by Keyondra Lockett
- o "Dirt" by Mary Mary
- o "I Was Here" by Beyoncé
- o "I'll Keep My Faith" by MAJOR

CHAPTER 9

Pay It Forward

⌒⌒⌒

Every day we wake up, we have an opportunity to make a difference and impact those around us. It is through our actions that we can offer support, encouragement, and help others reach their destiny. Whenever I can impart my knowledge and bring happiness into someone's life, I don't take it lightly. I want to pour into everyone by sharing my experiences and reassure them that they can achieve whatever their heart desires. As they sought after their dreams, they will soon realize that it will take determination, passion, dedication, and perseverance to get to where they want to go.

In early April 2014, I decided that I'd go visit my high school since I was on spring break from my first year of college. It had been nearly two years since I last saw some of my former teachers and friends, and I wanted to just hang out with them for the entire day. I emailed Mrs. Bowlds a week earlier and told her that I would be coming. She replied with such excitement and said, "I can't wait to see you. I'll let everyone know." She also wanted me to talk to a couple of students about college life, my own experiences, and give words of encouragement and advice. I had no idea that this trip would turn out to be something more.

The bus dropped me off at the main entrance around 9:00 a.m., I waited by the front desk and one of the security guards called Mrs. Bowlds to tell her that I had arrived. A few moments later, there she was with the biggest smile on her face. As we were headed toward the classroom, she revealed that she really wanted me to speak with my friend Melissa whom I have known since elementary school who, like me, is a wheelchair user too. The thought of reconnecting with her made me smile. Mrs. Bowlds went on to say that Melissa had a few questions about college she wanted me to answer. Then she said, "I think you would be a wonderful mentor to her. She looks up to you so much." As she was saying these words to me, so many thoughts were going through my mind. First, *I didn't know that she felt that way.* Second, *I never mentored anyone before. I mean, I always encouraged her daily while in school, but I did not think that was enough to be a mentor.* Third, *What do I say or what should I say?* I wanted to express something meaningful that she would appreciate as well as motivate and encourage her. I've come across so many people, even friends, who have felt they are unworthy or unable to pursue a college education because of their disability. I know that it's not true, and that's why I made it my mission before I left that school to share my own experiences and leave her with a piece of advice that she could use throughout her life and beyond.

It was around 10:15 a.m. I was waiting for Melissa to get out of class. Suddenly, I heard her wheelchair getting closer and closer. As her aid helped drive her chair inside the classroom, she was so jovial and excited to see me. I felt the same way since we hadn't seen each other in a while. It felt wonderful to catch up and see how she was doing. An hour and a half later, I went with her to lunch, and we got the opportunity to talk a little bit more. She wanted to know more about my college experience so that she could get a glimpse of what to expect. She asked, "How was your transition from high school to college?" I replied by telling her that "college was a different atmosphere." What I meant by that was you have a lot of responsibility as a college student. You choose your own class schedule, you are responsible for reading all the materials that the professor assigns, and you decide how many classes you take. When it comes to obtaining your college degree, it is up to you to put in the work because no one is going to do it for you. In high school, teachers are constantly making sure that you are staying on top of everything and checking to see if your homework is complete. Once you start college, you don't have that luxury anymore.

Melissa then asked, "What happens if you drop something or need something out of your bookbag?" I smiled and said, "I usually asked a student sitting next to me in class, or if I see someone walking by in the hallway, I'll ask them. It definitely took me some time to get used to. I recall my first day of college, sitting in English 101. I already had my textbook and materials because my mom took them out for me. After being there for almost an hour, my professor began wrapping up his lecture, and class was coming to an end. I realized that I needed my other textbook and notebook for my next class. My mom wasn't there, so that meant I had to ask one of my classmates for help, but one thing was blocking my request—my shyness. It also didn't help that I didn't know anyone in the class. I wanted to hide under a rock. When I got ready to open my mouth, no words came out. I tried again. Nothing. I saw a classmate who sat next to me packing up his belongings. I knew I needed to say something. Then, after silently encouraging myself, *C'mon Jennifer, you can do it*, I asked him, and he said, "Sure." The first two weeks of the semester, I was skeptical about asking him because I was unsure of how he'd react. I also didn't want him to feel like I was burdening him. Surprisingly, that never happened. He kindly gave me what I asked for. As time progressed, we became friends, and I didn't even have to ask him! He'd say, "Do you want me to get your books for you?" I'd say yes. Once he gave them to me, he always asked if I needed anything else. I smiled and said, "No, thank you," and we parted ways.

Entering a new phase in our lives can be scary. One of the main reasons is that we aren't sure of what to expect. Therefore, we fear that we will be alone and won't be successful. But, when we take a moment to breathe, slow down, trust ourselves, and embrace the journey, everything will start to align. Just like how I learned to make friends in high school and asked for help in college. You can do the same. All you need is a little faith to carry you through. I knew that my friend needed a confidence boost, so when Mrs. Bowlds asked, "Jen, what advice would you give to her for when she begins college?" I replied, "Stay focused on your goal and what you want. You must work hard. If you can accomplish those two important things, then I have no doubt in my mind that you will succeed in college. While pursuing your degree, you might face a few challenges along the way, but you do not let it distract you from your goals." She smiled and thanked me. Mrs. Bowlds said, "That was great advice." She finished up her lunch, and we all went back to homeroom. I stayed with her for the rest of the day until my mom picked me up. What was once a simple trip to my high school to visit some former teachers and friends on my spring break turned into something even more beautiful and profound. I got the opportunity to mentor one of my good friends and enlighten her about college life. She got a glimpse of what it is like to be a college student, and I was able to use my life as an example and to let her know that there is no limit to your disability. You can achieve whatever your heart desires. You just must put forth the effort and believe in yourself.

A year later, Melissa came to tour the same community college that I was attending with some other students. I was there that day, taking classes. Jessie and I met her in the cafeteria later for a quick chat—just like when we last saw each other. As she was telling me about her experience, she seemed much more confident about starting this new chapter in her life. I was beaming with excitement because I always knew in my heart that she had what it took to accomplish her goals. Even when she went off to college, we kept in touch, and I continued to encourage her along the way. Honestly, it never crossed my mind how much of an impact I had on her. I'm thankful we got to spend those moments together and I couldn't be prouder of her. Keep going, friend! You've got this.

How are you using your life to help others? It is so important to encourage, motivate, or lend a hand because someone might be searching for it. They could have been going through a tough time, and your presence made them smile. I want to remind you to be an example for those around you because you never know whose life you are impacting. Sometimes you might even think that you don't have anything to contribute, but everybody can bless somebody. When you do pay it forward, it doesn't always have to be on a grand scale. It can be as simple as writing an appreciation letter, sending flowers or a kind text message, offering to buy a meal, giving a hug, asking about their day, or taking the time to listen to their thoughts and feelings. Even if you only touch a few people or one person, they will never forget what you did for them or how you made them feel. In Mary Mary's song "God Bless," they sing about the importance of being a blessing to others. Whenever we are given the chance to make people smile or encourage their hearts, we must not turn away because our kind words and sweet gestures could be the remedy to helping them rediscover who they are and unlock their true purpose.

God's Grace Kept Me Playlist

Doesn't it feel wonderful when you are able to brighten someone's day and inspire him or her to be the best person he or she can be? Here are a couple of songs to remind you to always spread love and kindness to others.

- o "Never Lost" by Cece Winans
- o "Friend in Me" by The Walls Group
- o "Don't Go Alone" by Brennen John
- o "Brighter Days" by Emeli Sande

CHAPTER 10

Turning Rejection into Resilience

Rejection can be hard. It is not something that we can shake off or forget about easily. Even though we try our best to conceal our emotions, we still hurt on the inside. As time passes, we begin to feel like a failure or that we just aren't good enough. We replay everything in our minds, trying to figure out what went wrong or how we could have made the situation better. After so long, we eventually shut down, stop believing in ourselves, and wonder if we truly belong. I've had my share of instances where I felt like I didn't quite "fit in," and I often wondered whether something was wrong with me. Then I realized I can no longer dwell on situations that I can't change or allow disappointment to hold me back from pursuing my goals. All I can do is focus on the present, believe I will rise above every challenge, and understand that I will come out stronger than ever.

It was just like any other day in college. I entered through the doors with my books on my tray, waited for the elevator, and headed to class. While waiting for the professor to arrive, three friends sat in the front of the classroom. They were always together and commented on every discussion. As for me, I never really said anything to anyone—not in this class anyway. On this day, two of the ladies were talking to each other, and another classmate responded. She turned around, laughed, and engaged with him. So, I thought I'd join in the conversation too—just to see what would happen. When I responded, the room went quiet. She was silent. She didn't even acknowledge me. She and her friend both stared at each other, then ended the conversation abruptly. She didn't utter one word. Some days, she and her friends would speak to me passing through the hallway. But why was this time different? "Does she not want to be judged for talking to me? Am I only good enough to talk to her when no one is around? My smile quickly disappeared, and I got a disheartening feeling in my chest. "You knew that this was going to happen, Jennifer." In the back of my mind, I knew that I'd probably receive a not so friendly reaction. Yet, I wanted her to prove me wrong. I was holding out hope that she'd eventually turn around and interact with me, but it did not turn out that that way.

Sometimes when we experience rejection, we have difficulty accepting the truth. Even if it's right in front of our faces, we choose to ignore the signs because we think it'll eventually change. We so desperately try to fix the situation that we sacrifice our own happiness. While we are constantly worrying and losing sleep over what they have done, they aren't pondering about how their actions have affected or afflicted pain on us. Yet, we keep quiet and continue pressing on. Why? Maybe we are willing to accept the pain to feel validated and valued by others. We also desire to always see the good in others. It's just natural for us to still want to see potential in others after they have proven themselves otherwise.

That's essentially what I did with my classmate and her friends. I only saw what I wanted to see, which was a fantasy that I created through my own imagination. I believed that I was making myself feel better, but in fact I was trying to cover up my wounded heart by suppressing my emotions. I couldn't escape because all my classes were with them. We even had to do a presentation together, and all went great, but I still felt uncomfortable. I had reached a point in the semester when I didn't want to attend classes anymore because I knew they'd be there. I just wanted this nightmare to end. About a month was left of school when I decided that I couldn't go on feeling sorry for myself anymore. I had to make a choice. *Jennifer, you can continue to be miserable, or you can pick yourself up and focus on finishing the semester strong.* I didn't have to think twice about it. I stopped concentrating on my classmates and began putting myself first. That was the best choice I ever made! I felt happier than I have in months and my mind was clearer. I came to the realization that I'm just trying to obtain my degree like everyone else.

I finally made it to the end of the semester, and we were having a potluck party to celebrate. I was sitting at the table toward the back of the classroom. I saw people eating food and just talking to one another. Then I saw her having a conversation in the corner with a few classmates. When I looked up again, she was standing right next to me. Since I was not talking to anyone, and she wasn't near her friends, she must've felt compelled to talk to me. Suddenly, she said with a cheerful look on her face, "Hi, Jennifer." I'm thinking, *You're talking to me today! Just a few days ago, you gave me the cold shoulder and pretended like I didn't exist. I could do the same to you, but I won't. I'm still going to speak.* You can say that I get it from my mom because no matter if someone talked badly about her or did her wrong, she would still speak when she saw him or her. My mom instilled in me to never hold grudges and to keep the peace but speak up when necessary. She also believed that being hostile takes up too much time and energy when we can all just move on. My mom often says, "I'm going to feed them with a long-handled spoon." What my mom meant was that she will be cordial and not let anyone or any disagreement interfere with her happiness.

Sometimes I would get annoyed when I felt she should've said something. But I realized that in each of those moments, she was helping me. She was helping me understand that not everything is worth our time. We must choose our battles wisely and be mindful of our actions toward others. However, if we did feel strongly about an issue, she encouraged us to never be afraid to voice our opinion. Well, on this day, I took a page from my mom's book. I politely smiled at her and spoke back. It felt good, and I went on to finish the semester strong just like I promised.

I know it might sound a bit strange, but I felt like I won! I won a battle that I was once scared to confront and did it my way. Let's be clear, this wasn't about making friends. It was more about realizing that I am in control of my own narrative. How I react to a situation ultimately shapes the outcome. Yes, it's true that I could've treated her with the same amount of decency that she showed me, but I chose to take the high road and still be kind. I firmly believe that fighting fire with fire never solves anything. While it might feel good to bring others down when you're disappointed and bitter, you'll discover that all you've created is just a *huge* mess! Then, you are left trying to pick up the pieces. That's what I didn't want to do, but I did almost allow my perception of what I wanted make me lose sight of my goal. The moment I unselfishly began focusing on me and the things that matter most, I started winning. I became resilient. I desire for you to begin tapping into your own resilience! It's in there, but to obtain it, you must decide what you want for your life. No one can do it for you. It's also important for you to understand that you don't have to settle for less than your worth. You deserve to be happy and need to start living again! Jessica Reedy's song "Keep It Moving" simply reminds us that no matter what we go through in life, we must hold our head up high and continue to smile. There's a whole world waiting for you to shine, to sprinkle your magic, and to show them what you've got! Now I'd like to share with you some takeaways from the chapter. You can highlight or write them down in your journal.

* When people show you who they are, believe them.
* Be kind to yourself even when things aren't going as planned.
* Learn to accept what you cannot change and move on.
* Sometimes what we want is not always what we need or what's best.

* Every battle is not worth fighting. Make sure you choose them wisely and carefully.
* It is not always about what someone did but how you respond.
* Never let anything or anyone stand in the way of your happiness.
* Start letting go of people who bring you down or don't add value to your life.
* Some people come into your life to remind you of how powerful you are.
* The moment you take back your power, you begin to fully own who you are.

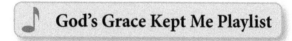

God's Grace Kept Me Playlist

If you ever need to be reminded of your resilience, here's some of my favorite songs that will help you find yourself again and unleash your electrifying superpower.

o "Trouble Ain't" by Mary Mary
o "Lava" by Danni Baylor
o "Ready Enough" by Sidibe
o "Shine Bright" by MAJOR

CHAPTER 11

No One Does It Alone

No one reaches the peak of success on their own. While discovering who we are and finding our ultimate purpose, there was someone or something that influenced, guided, and inspired us to strive toward greatness. It could have been a mentor who gave you hope. Maybe your children encouraged you when you were on the verge of giving up. You might have come across a powerful message that made you feel empowered, or perhaps you listened to a song, and the lyrics resonated with your soul so deeply that you found yourself again. As we forge ahead on our journeys, it's important to acknowledge and show love to those who have supported us through it all, reminded us of our courageousness, and paved the way for us to thrive.

By this time, I'd already obtained my associate's degree in English and got accepted to a four-year university. When I was pursuing my bachelor's degree at twenty-three, I set a goal that I was going to finish within one year. I wanted to challenge myself. I asked my adviser, Dr. Smith, how long it would take me to complete the program. He kindly told my mom and me, while we were sitting in his office, "You'll probably be done in four years." *Oh no, no, no,* I thought. He didn't know this, but in my mind, I had mapped out how to accomplish my goal. I also held on to the advice that Mrs. Thompson had given me during my community college days. She said, "It's the student's responsibility to always keep track of their degree progress." Her words forever stuck with me, which was why I was constantly checking my study plan to make sure that I registered for all the right classes. I even calculated my credits each semester to see how much further I had left to go. Ever had a person tell you something, but you believed in your heart that you could achieve more and was determined to get it done? This was my mindset from the start. I knew that achieving this goal was not going to be easy, but I was ready to dive right in!

I started out with five classes but then began taking at least six to seven classes per semester. (Yeah, I know, a lot of studying and discipline). At times, I thought that I was in over my head, like, *What did I get myself into?* But the one person who always stood in my corner was my mom. She was there for me. Sometimes I'd take the bus to school, and she'd pick me up or vice versa. If for whatever reason there was a hiccup in our routine, she'd stop what she was doing to make sure I had everything I needed. Every time I would get in the car after school, she'd always ask, "How was school today, Jenny?" I replied, "It was good." She would listen to me talk about my day, we'd laugh, have heart-to-heart conversations, and we often stopped for vanilla milkshakes from McDonald's before we got home. I appreciated those car rides so much—they always made my heart happy and still do.

Toward the end of the semester, I had to write a fifteen- to twenty-page paper and create a presentation for Dr. Muhammad's class. I was in the final stretch, and graduation seemed so close yet so far away. I was working on this paper for a while, but I felt like I was not at my best. I had a strong topic, but several pieces were missing. I stayed cooped up in my room trying to get this paper off the ground, but nothing was going as planned. While typing on my laptop, I realized that I had only written four pages. I was constantly deleting sentences and so forth. I felt so defeated because I had a long way to go, and the deadline was approaching fast. I was stressing out because Dr. Muhammad had such high expectations, and I just wanted to make her proud and receive an excellent grade. I was so overwhelmed that I started to think that I was not going to graduate. I took a minute to collect myself and breathe. I said, "OK, Jennifer, you can do this." Then, I started to pray and ask God to give me strength to make it through this process. I needed help and desired for Him to lead me in the right direction. Later that night, around ten o'clock amid writing my last thoughts before bed, my mom came into my room and asked, "How's your paper going, Jenny?" I took a break from writing and said, "Mom, I don't think I'm going to make it." She replied with a smile, "You can do this, boo. You're almost there."

We all need someone to talk to, whether it's calling your best friend to chat about your day or reaching out to a loved one for some encouraging words. Either way, we can rely on those relationships to make us laugh when we feel down, comfort us when we are crying, and offer support when life becomes overwhelming. I want you to think about a time when you felt like life was caving in around you. Maybe you felt your life was falling apart, or you'd reached a point where you felt you couldn't go on. The moment you thought everything was on the right track, you end up back where you started. Just when you are about to give up and end it all, something happens that brings you back from the edge. What saved you? Was God whispering in your ear? Did you envision a friend or someone you admire speaking to your heart? Were you suddenly humming a melody to one of your favorite songs? Whatever helped you out of that dark place, just stay there, and meditate for a minute. When you're ready, open your eyes. Do you feel revitalized? Sometimes all it takes is that one moment to change our lives forever.

When my mom spoke those words to me, that's how I felt. It was just something about the way she said it that made me leap into action and start to believe in myself again. It is as if she knew exactly what to say to encourage me to keep going. She saw my potential and wanted to see her daughter soar. A few weeks later, I found out that I passed the class, and I graduated with my bachelor's degree in English, something I worked extremely hard for. Most of all, I did it all in one year. My family and friends (especially my mom) were rooting for me every step of the way.

So, what person has been very supportive in your life? Occasionally, we must take the time to express gratitude toward the people who have been there for us through our setbacks, obstacles, accomplishments, and major milestones. Let them know that you care and what they mean to you. They might not have known just how much they were loved and appreciated. Life is short. We must be intentional about celebrating the individuals that made it possible for us to succeed and do what we love. I feel extremely blessed to have people in my circle who genuinely want the best for me and support all my endeavors. I understand what a difference that has made in my life—one of the reasons why I started JMotivates is so that I can affirm and encourage others. No one needs to walk alone. We must learn to thank the people we have, proactively work to build our positive community, and make sure to pass on the encouragement to the next person we meet.

♪ God's Grace Kept Me Playlist

During those quiet moments when you begin to feel alone, I pray the messages in each of these songs remind you of how many people love, cherish, and appreciate having you in their lives.

- o "Count on You" by the Walls Group
- o "Just Hold On" by Jelinda Hill
- o "You Are Not Alone" by Emeli Sandé
- o "Because You Loved Me" By Celine Dion
- o "I'm With You/Be Still" by Israel Houghton ft. Adrienne Houghton

CHAPTER 12

You Are Exactly Where God Wants You to Be

Many of us have been in a place where we've sat with our thoughts trying to figure out which direction we should take. It can be a difficult and confusing time. On the one hand, we have an idea of what we want but aren't sure of how to get there. We might also feel that we are at a standstill and awaiting confirmation from God. Sometimes we have people around us who don't fully understand the nature of our assignment here on earth, which causes us to overthink, second-guess our choices, and believe that we aren't where we're supposed to be on our journey. But we often forget that God is in control. He places us where He sees fit, even if we are unable to see the blessing for ourselves.

Some people have tried to put a damper on my dreams or tell me what I should be doing with my life. When those situations occurred, I started thinking that I'd made a mistake or that I was not good enough. I'd say to myself, *Maybe they're right. If only I had tried a little bit harder, things would be a lot different.* Some years ago, I was talking to someone who I admired deeply. I was twenty-four at the time, and we were discussing my recent accomplishments and future aspirations. Our conversation was going great until the person said to me, "You could have been walking on your own too by now, if you would've done what you were supposed to do." In that moment, it was as if everything stopped and time just stood still. I was wondering, *Where did this comment come from? Why would you say that?* I could feel myself starting to shut down. I didn't want to talk anymore. The only thing I wanted was to be left alone.

I could never seem to understand why the person always brought up this subject almost every time we talked. *Is that all you see when you look at me … the fact that I'm not walking on my own yet?* It felt like no matter what I'd accomplished in my life, that person chose to only focus on this aspect. What hurt the most wasn't the comments but that it was coming from someone who I thought would always support me through everything. Someone who I believed would ride the wave with me.

A couple weeks later, my mom and I were sitting in the car having a conversation. I was explaining to her how so many people seem to always zoom in on what you aren't doing, instead of what you've done. She then said, "People can't predict the future." I agreed with her and said, "There is a reason for everything. There is a reason why God wanted me to be in a wheelchair. Perhaps He desires for me to help and encourage other wheelchair users as well." She replied, "Exactly." When we finished talking, I felt so relieved and optimistic to see all the wonderful opportunities God has planned for my future.

If you don't mind, I want to take a few minutes to encourage your heart. You are where you are because God placed you there for a reason. For such a long time, I didn't quite understand why God allowed me to go through certain situations. It took me years to recognize that when I was faced with hardships, God was testing me. He was testing to see if I was ready to enter the next phase. He put me through a series of exams for my heart, mind, body, and soul and carefully analyzed the results. If everything came back negative, then I was in the clear. But if the results were positive, then I had some work to do. While working on getting better, God also put me in a waiting season until He felt like I was well-equipped to fulfill His plan. Maybe you are anxious and anticipating for God to give you the green light. Don't worry, it's coming. I don't know when … you just must be patient and trust His timing! God is setting the stage for something magical. Once He unveils His plan, you will be prepared to receive all the blessings that God has for you!

I'd also like to speak to the people who are letting the opinions of others weigh them down and making them believe they're not doing enough. I've been right where they are—feeling obligated to do what those around me want out of fear of hurting them, scared to say how I feel because of what people might say or think, and sacrificing my own happiness to please others. That's a tough spot to be in, but I had to learn that I can't live my life according to my friends or family. I must live for Jennifer and trust the path that God has for me. Now, I challenge you to start living for you, follow your heart, and keep God in the center of everything that you do. Some of you are probably thinking that's easier said than done, but I'm here to let you know it's possible. You don't have to do anything that doesn't satisfy you. If you feel that what you're doing is no longer serving you, making you unhappy, and not helping you reach your purpose, then you shouldn't be doing it, and you can walk away. You might be afraid to let go because you don't want to disappoint anyone, but I'm encouraging you to take that leap of faith. You'll never know what can happen until you try.

Sometimes you also must drown out the background noise. Not everyone is looking out for your best interest and not every piece of advice is beneficial for where you're trying to go. If there are people in your life who never have anything nice to say, discourage you from following your dreams, etc., then they are not on your team. We spend a lot of time worrying about what others are saying, but the real question we should be asking ourselves is this: "What does God say?" God will always be on our side. One of the most amazing things I love about God is how He wants to see us win. When we need to talk, God listens. If we have a problem, He helps us come up with solutions. God is there for us no matter what, so why don't we trust Him? Why aren't we showing up for Him like He does for us every day? It's time we stop internalizing all the negative energy, reconnect with God, and allow Him to guide us toward our destination.

I have not given up on my dream of walking by myself one day. In fact, I think about that quite often. More often than people might realize, but I come to trust and lean into God's timing. As I said earlier, no one knows the future. I'm still stretching daily and doing things to stay strong. It's a part of the process, and I believe the only way to become stronger is to keep working at it. Most importantly, I know in my heart that God will continue to cover me on my journey. I've gained so much knowledge from this experience. After I reveal to you what I've learned, my prayer is that you will begin to see that you are exactly where God wants you to be.

* What people say to you can't be how you define or see yourself.
* People have a way of looking at you through the lens of lack.
* Many will always zero in on what's not done, instead of what you've already achieved. That is their issue, and it has no bearing on your story.
* Everything that we experience in life, God uses as teachable moments to help us grow into our purpose.
* God will never steer you wrong. He will take you places that you would've never imagined.
* What God has for you is yours, and nobody can take it away.
* Start listening to what God says about you. He is always thinking of ways for you to flourish.

I feel like this message hits home for so many of you reading this right now. I'm sure you all have experienced doubts on your journey and wondered if you're on the right path. The short answer is yes. God doesn't put us in situations just for fun. It's a way for Him to educate and give us key instructions so that we can live a prosperous life. I don't know about you, but I refuse to quit. I'm going to continue to trust God and wait patiently until my time arrives. Will you join me? I hope so! You've come so far already, and I don't want you to quit on yourself or your dreams. You're too remarkable for that! Whenever you start to feel like you are falling behind, just have faith that God has everything under control.

 God's Grace Kept Me Playlist

One day while talking to one of my mentors, I was having a moment. I was being hard on myself because even though I accomplished many of my goals, I still felt like I wasn't where I thought I should be in my life. She stopped me and said, "Jennifer, you won't always have high moments. There will be days when you feel low, and that's okay. We all have them." She taught me to trust the process and to enjoy every part of my journey. So, I want to leave you with this message. God knows exactly what He is doing, and you will get there soon enough. Take some time to yourself and soak it all in. You just might learn something amazing! While you are waiting for God to promote you to the next level, why don't you listen to a few songs from my playlist! They will bring you peace and remind you of what happens when you stop worrying and leave it to God.

- o "It Is Well" by Mary Mary
- o "I've Got Joy" by CeCe Winans
- o "And You Don't Stop" by The Walls Group
- o "Going" by Christina Bell
- o "I Belong Here" by Rudy Currence

Moving Forward with Grace

What an exhilarating and incredible ride this has been! We've weathered many storms, faced our fears, and overcame numerous obstacles together. Now our journey has come to an end. But I know that I would not have gotten through any of these experiences if weren't for God's grace—carrying me through time and time again. When I reflect on my life and all I've had to endure, I feel extremely grateful to still be here. Still smiling. Still believing. Still keeping the faith. Still shining my light. Still fulfilling my purpose.

And guess what? You're still here too, working hard on your goals and pursuing your passion! I'm so proud of you for never giving up, for continuing to persevere, and for giving yourself permission to evolve into the person you've always wanted to be. I pray that as you read my story, something deeply resonated with you or pushed you to not only step outside of the box but to create your own. Whether you've built a big or a small box, the size doesn't matter. If the box fits your standards, and you're happy, then it's perfect. You set the tone for how you desire to live your life, and you should let nothing or no one get in the way of your dreams.

As you begin your next chapter, I want you to move forward with grace. Let God propel you toward your destiny. Step into your purpose confidently and elegantly. If at any point, you start to lose focus and need to readjust, God will lead you back to your rightful place. When life starts to become tough, and you aren't sure if you can withstand or remain hopeful, think about how often God has kept you. He has saved us more than we can count. Even when we don't always deserve it, He continues to bless us anyway. Isn't God just amazing?! I'm beyond thankful that I got to spend time with each of you. I'm even more excited to see all the extraordinary things that you accomplish in the future. I can't wait to celebrate you and all your success. Stay connected with me on Instagram at JMotivates as we continue motivating, sending encouragement, inspiring, empowering, and uplifting each other daily. Never stop shining your light. Always remember, whatever you do, do it with grace.